Baby Animals in the Wild!

Skunk Kits in the Wild

by Katie Chanez

Bullfrog Books

Ideas for Parents and Teachers

Bullfrog Books let children practice reading informational text at the earliest reading levels. Repetition, familiar words, and photo labels support early readers.

Before Reading

- Discuss the cover photo. What does it tell them?

- Look at the picture glossary together. Read and discuss the words.

Read the Book

- "Walk" through the book and look at the photos. Let the child ask questions. Point out the photo labels.

- Read the book to the child, or have him or her read independently.

After Reading

- Prompt the child to think more. Ask: Skunk kits have stripes. Can you name other animals that have stripes?

Bullfrog Books are published by Jump!
5357 Penn Avenue South
Minneapolis, MN 55419
www.jumplibrary.com

Library of Congress Cataloging-in-Publication Data

Names: Chanez, Katie, author.
Title: Skunk kits in the wild / by Katie Chanez.
Description: Minneapolis, MN: Jump!, Inc., [2024]
Series: Baby animals in the wild! | Includes index.
Audience: Ages 5–8
Identifiers: LCCN 2022046126 (print)
LCCN 2022046127 (ebook)
ISBN 9798885244152 (hardcover)
ISBN 9798885244169 (paperback)
ISBN 9798885244176 (ebook)
Subjects: LCSH: Skunks—Infancy—Juvenile literature.
Classification: LCC QL737.C248 C43 2024 (print)
LCC QL737.C248 (ebook)
DDC 599.76/81392—dc23/eng/20221223
LC record available at https://lccn.loc.gov/2022046126
LC ebook record available at https://lccn.loc.gov/2022046127

Editor: Eliza Leahy
Designer: Molly Ballanger

Photo Credits: Don Johnston/All Canada Photos/SuperStock, cover, 5, 6–7, 23tl, 23tr; Nynke van Holten/Shutterstock, 1, 3 (right), 11, 22; Chris Brignell/Dreamstime, 3 (left); Wayne Lynch/All Canada Photos/SuperStock, 4, 23bl; KenCanning/iStock, 8–9; blickwinkel/Alamy, 10; Geoffrey Kuchera/Dreamstime, 12–13; Josef Pittner/Shutterstock, 14; Lynn_Bystrom/iStock, 15; Danita Delimont/Shutterstock, 16–17; Animals Animals/SuperStock, 18–19; Holly Kuchera/Shutterstock, 20–21; Vangelis_Vassalakis/Shutterstock, 23br; reptiles4all/iStock, 24.

Printed in the United States of America at Corporate Graphics in North Mankato, Minnesota.

Table of Contents

Stinky Spray

It is spring.
Skunk kits are born!

kit

This log is their den.
Mom keeps them safe.

Mom

Skunk kits have black fur.
They have white stripes.
They have bushy tails.

tail

stripe

7

The kits follow Mom.
She carries one.

They look for food.
They dig for bugs.

claw

They use their claws.

They find fruit.
Yum!

A kit lifts its tail.

It sprays a smelly liquid.

The coyote runs away.

The kits are safe!

It is fall.

The kits stay with Mom through winter.

Spring is here again. The kits are all grown up.

They leave to find their own dens.

Parts of a Skunk Kit

What are the parts of a skunk kit? Take a look!

tail

ear

fur

paw

claw

nose

Picture Glossary

bushy
Thick and fluffy.

den
The home of a wild animal.

kits
Baby skunks.

liquid
A substance that flows and can
be poured or sprayed.

Index

To Learn More

Finding more information is as easy as 1, 2, 3.

❶ Go to www.factsurfer.com

❷ Enter "skunkkits" into the search box.

❸ Choose your book to see a list of websites.